HARRY + Catherine Timmy

ENJOY o

Jim O.

"I NEVER COULD STAND LOSING, SECOND PLACE DIDN'T INTEREST ME."

—Ty Cobb

Stewart, Tabori & Chang
New York

# 101 Reasons to Love the TIGERS™

## David Green

# Introduction

Perhaps former Tigers manager Sparky Anderson said it best: "All Detroiters aren't sports fans, but all Detroiters love the Tigers."

Baseball has a way of embedding itself in the fabric of a community, and the Tigers and the city of Detroit are as intertwined as any in sports—each breathing life into the other, sharing the good times and the bad, decade after decade.

From the early part of the 20th century, when the city was booming and the population soared as the automobile industry exploded, the Tigers shared in the success, winning three American League pennants in a row, from 1907 to 1909.

When the country grappled with depression in the 1930s and bitter disputes between labor unions and automakers threatened to rip the city apart, the Tigers revived the city's spirits with a pennant in 1934 and their first world championship, in 1935.

With the specter of World War II looming, the Tigers brought home another AL pennant in 1940. Detroit became known as "the arsenal of democracy" as it shifted its manufacturing focus to military equipment. Just weeks after the offical end of the war, the Tigers added a second world championship, in 1945.

In 1967, in the midst of "the Summer of Love," riots rocked Newark and Detroit, leaving 43 dead in the Motor City. The Tigers battled doggedly throughout the summer and early fall, only to fall one game short of the pennant that year. But they reunited a wounded, divided city and brought dancing to the streets when they won their third World Series title the following year.

The 1980s saw more and more residents fleeing the city for the suburbs, leaving many of the downtown buildings abandoned, left to crumble. But at "The Corner," the Tigers kept hope alive. In 1984, the Tigers had their greatest season ever, winning a fourth World Series title, and once again reviving the city.

Then, after more than a decade of forgettable baseball, with Detroit struggling more than ever to maintain its position as the center of the automobile industry, out of nowhere the Tigers put together yet another championship season, winning the American League pennant in 2006, and restoring pride and respect to a tarnished franchise and city.

Different teams take on different personas over the years. And for more than a century, the Tigers have traditionally been viewed as a blue-collar team in a blue-collar town. A hard-working, lunch pail-toting, dirt-under-their fingernails team that has captured the hearts of the everyday folk in Detroit, throughout Michigan, and well beyond. And isn't that how it should be?

"THE GREAT AMERICAN GAME SHOULD BE AN UNRELENTING WAR OF NERVES."

—Ty Cobb

COBB, DETROIT

1907 World Series, Detroit versus
Chicago at Bennett Park

# 1 Birth of the Tigers

The birth of the American League can be traced to November 20, 1893, when the Western League, a minor-league association, reorganized after going bankrupt. Ban Johnson was elected president of the league, and when the National League went from 12 teams to eight in 1900, the Western League was renamed the American League and declared itself a major league in 1901. Detroit, a member of the Western League, then began its long, storied history as one of the original members of the American League.

Trolleys carrying fans to Navin Field in 1934

## 2 The Corner

The intersection of Michigan and Trumbell Avenues on the west side of downtown Detroit was the home of Detroit baseball for more than a century, from 1896 through 1999. Millions of fans over multiple generations made pilgrimages to "The Corner" to watch Tigers greats Ty Cobb, Charlie Gehringer, Hank Greenberg, Al Kaline, and all the rest play at Bennett Park, Navin Field, Briggs Stadium, and Tiger Stadium.

# 3 Bennett Park

Back in 1896, when the Tigers were part of the Western League, owner George Vanderbeck built a rickety wooden structure on what had been the Western Market and town dog pound at the corner of Michigan and Trumbull Avenues. The original park featured a small wooden grandstand that accommodated about 5,000 customers. The site was covered with elm trees, and when construction on the park began, Vanderbeck elected to leave eight of the trees in the outfield. In the first official Western League game played at the park, on April 28, 1896, Detroit topped Columbus 17–2. The park was named after Charlie Bennett, a former catcher for the 1880s National League Detroit Wolverines who had lost a leg and a foot in a train accident. Bennett Park would be home to the Tigers until 1911, when it was razed to be replaced by Navin Field.

Bennett Park, circa 1900

# 4 Starting Strong

After a rainout postponed opening day in 1901, the Tigers played their first official game as a major-league team on April 25, 1901. Things did not go well early for the Detroit nine, and the Tigers trailed the Milwaukee Brewers 13–4 going into the bottom of the ninth at Bennett Park. Then, to the delight of the home crowd, Detroit exploded with 10 runs in the final frame to shock the Brewers 14–13.

# 5 The Tigers

The exact origin of their name is unclear, but the team has been known as the Tigers since 1895. Manager George Stallings took credit for the name after having the team wear black and orange socks, similar to those worn by the Princeton Tigers, but records indicate the name was in use before Stallings was managing the team, in 1901.

# 6 The Olde English D

The unmistakable "D" that adorns Detroit's home jerseys and caps is the oldest logo currently in use in professional sports. The D originally was a part of the Tigers' uniforms when they were in the Western League. With the exception of a few years in the late 1920s and early 1930s, as well as 1960, the D has been part of the AL club's uniforms since 1904. There are subtle differences between the D used on the Tigers' caps and the one on the jersey, which apparently is due to different companies being involved in the manufacturing process over the years. If trying to choose which is better, the jersey D seems to have the upper hand, having been the same on all four World Series–winning uniforms.

Germany Schaefer tries his hand as photographer instead of subject while a member of the Washington Senators.

# 7 Herman the Great

Crowd favorite Germany Schaefer, when asked to pinch-hit during a game in 1906, announced to the Chicago fans as he approached the batter's box that he was "Herman the Great, acknowledged by one and all to be the greatest hitter in the world," and informed the crowd that he would homer into the left-field bleachers. He did, then proceeded to slide headfirst into each base, adding colorful commentary as he went. When he slid into home, Schaefer jumped to his feet and proclaimed, "Schaefer wins by a nose!"

# 8 Take Me Out to the Ball Game

The vaudeville act of Tigers teammates Germany Schaefer and Charley O'Leary was the inspiration for the 1949 MGM musical *Take Me Out to the Ball Game*, starring Frank Sinatra and Gene Kelly.

# 9 Davy Jones

Jones patrolled the outfield with Ty Cobb and Sam Crawford. In his seven years as a Tiger, from 1906 to 1912, Jones stole 140 bases without ever being caught. In fact, he never was caught in 207 attempts throughout his 15-year major-league career.

# 10 The Boss

Charles "Boss" Schmidt, a catcher with the Tigers from 1906 through 1911, was said to have fists of granite, and legend has it that he could pound nails into the floor with those fists. He once fought heavyweight boxing champion Jack Johnson in an exhibition match and was widely considered to be the toughest man in baseball.

Fans gather outside Detroit City Hall to watch the scoreboard in 1908 as the Tigers capture their second AL pennant.

# 11 Three in a Row

The Tigers won their first American League pennant in 1907, edging the Philadelphia Athletics by a game and a half. It was the first of three consecutive pennants for the Detroit nine. Led by emerging star Ty Cobb, the Tigers took on the Chicago Cubs in the World Series. Game 1 ended in a 3–3 tie, called after 12 innings because of darkness. It would be the closest Detroit would come to victory, as the Cubs' pitching shut down the Tigers' bats, and Chicago went on to sweep the next four games.

The following year featured a rematch of the 1907 World Series. The Tigers had won the AL pennant on the last day of the season and were determined to avenge their loss to the Cubs the previous year. In Game 1, the Tigers rallied to take a 6–5 lead into the ninth, but the Cubs scored five in the top of the ninth to steal the win. After Chicago won Game 2, 6–1, the Tigers finally recorded their first World Series victory, clubbing the Cubs 8–3 in Game 3. But, as in 1907, Chicago's pitchers shut down the Tigers' bats once again, and the Cubs won Games 4 and 5 in shutouts, claiming their second consecutive title.

Detroit raised its third straight AL pennant in 1909, but this time its World Series opponent was the Pittsburgh Pirates. The teams swapped victories through the first six games, with Tigers ace George Mullin picking up two victories, in Games 4 and 6. But Game 2 winner Wild Bill Donovan wasn't sharp in Game 7, and the Pirates swept to an 8–0 win, leaving the Tigers as bridesmaids for the third straight year.

# 12 20-Somethings

The 1907 pennant-winning Tigers featured three starting pitchers who won 20 or more games. Wild Bill Donovan led the way with a record of 25–4. Ed Killian went 25–13, and George Mullin was 20–20. It's the only time in Tigers history that they achieved the feat. In fact, only 23 teams in major-league history have had three or more 20-game winners, and none since the 1973 Oakland Athletics.

KILLIAN, DETROIT

DONOVAN, DETROIT

MULLIN, DETROIT

# 13 George Mullin

Mullin was a stalwart of the Tigers' pitching staff during the championship years of 1907–1909, winning a career-high 29 games in 1909. He started six games in three World Series and completed all six, with a 3–3 record. In his 12 seasons with the Tigers, from 1902 to 1913, Mullin won 20 or more games five times. Relying on an overpowering fastball and a multitude of tactics he used to distract hitters, such as scratching around the pitcher's mound while the batter waited, tying and retying his shoes, and even talking to the hitter, Mullin was able to win 209 games for Detroit, ranking him second all-time to Hooks Dauss. Mullin is the all-time leader in innings pitched for the Tigers with 3,394 and complete games with 336, and he threw the first no-hitter in Tigers history on July 4, 1912, versus the St. Louis Browns.

# 14 The Wild Pitch

As the story goes, during a game in the early 1900s, the Tigers were leading the New York Highlanders 1–0 in the bottom of the ninth, but the Highlanders had put a man on third with two outs. Catcher Charlie Schmidt made a trip to the mound to discuss the options with pitcher George Mullin. Schmidt came up with the crazy idea of having Mullin purposefully hurl a wild pitch over his head into the backstop, reasoning that the runner would break for home but Schmidt could retrieve the carom and fire to Mullin covering home for the out. Mullin thought he was crazy but decided to give it a try anyway. The men returned to their positions, Mullin made his pitch, and it bounced perfectly back to Schmidt, who then relayed it to Mullin to get the out and save the 1–0 win.

# 15 Hughie Jennings

Jennings, a Pennsylvania coal miner's son who graduated from Cornell with a law degree, was hired by Frank Navin to manage the Tigers starting in 1907. Under his leadership, the Tigers won consecutive American League pennants in Jennings' first three years at the helm, though they failed to win the World Series each year. Something of a showman, the crowd-pleasing Jennings often would encourage his team from his place in the coach's box by kicking his leg in the air and bellowing his trademark rallying cry, "Ee-yah!" Jennings also got along well with the notoriously prickly Ty Cobb by taking a hands-off approach, allowing Cobb to develop his extraordinary talent with only minimal guidance. Jennings' teams won 1,131 games during his 14-year tenure, ranking him second on the Tigers all-time list behind Sparky Anderson. Jennings was inducted into the National Baseball Hall of Fame in 1945.

"DO WHAT YOU THINK IS BEST AND I'LL BACK YOU UP."

—Hughie Jennings to Ty Cobb

Left to right: Matty McIntyre, Heinie Beckendorf, Davy Jones, Ed Killian, Sam Crawford, Ed Summers, George Winter, and Hugh Jennings leaving for spring training, circa 1909

# 16 Ty Cobb

Cobb was mean as a snake, ornery as a mule, a bristly, prickly, tormented man. But he was a baseball genius and possibly the greatest ever to play the game. Sure, many consider Babe Ruth to be the best ever, but Cobb was a smarter, more complete player. From the moment he first stepped into the batter's box in a Tigers uniform in 1905, doubling off future Hall of Famer Jack Chesbro, until his retirement in 1928 after spending his final two seasons in Philadelphia, "the Georgia Peach" dominated major-league baseball with his fierce, relentless aggressiveness. Cobb could hit with his eyes closed and ran the bases like no other, often intimidating the opposition into mistakes with his attacking style. The "genius in spikes" would outsmart his opponents, running when it wasn't expected and sliding hard into the bases, his razor-sharp spikes held high. Few, if any, of his teammates liked him, but all respected his unsurpassed abilities on the field.

Ironically, as great as he was, Cobb never won a World Series, reaching the Fall Classic three consecutive years from 1907 to 1909, then never returning. Cobb was player-manager of the team from 1921 to 1926, but his teams never finished higher than second. He was one of five original members of the National Baseball Hall of Fame, elected in 1936.

"THE GREATNESS OF TY COBB WAS SOMETHING
THAT HAD TO BE SEEN, AND TO SEE HIM WAS
TO REMEMBER HIM FOREVER."

—George Sisler

# 17 Cobb's Numbers

Ty Cobb's statistics are staggering. Many of his records are likely never to be broken.
- A lifetime batting average of .367
- Hit .320 or better for 23 consecutive years, in all but his first season in the majors
- Hit better than .400 three times, including .420 in 1911
- Led the American League in hitting 12 times
- His 4,191 hits are second only to Pete Rose
- His 2,245 runs scored are second to Rickey Henderson
- His 297 triples are second to fellow Tiger Sam Crawford
- He's fourth all-time in doubles and stolen bases with 723 and 892, respectively

# 18 One, Two, Three

Ty Cobb once stole second, third, and home on three consecutive pitches.

# 19 Oh, Brother!

After Ty Cobb was suspended for using his fists to silence a particularly abusive fan, his teammates staged a one-game strike in protest. So on May 18, 1912, instead of forfeiting the game, the Tigers fielded a makeshift team that included mostly college and semipro players, along with their 50-year-old coach, Deacon McGuire. Allan Travers, a student at St. Joseph's College in Philadelphia who later joined the priesthood, pitched a complete game for the Tigers, suffering a 24–2 loss at the hands of the Philadelphia Athletics, but received $50 for his effort.

"HUGHIE JENNINGS TOLD ME NOT TO THROW FASTBALLS AS HE WAS AFRAID I MIGHT GET KILLED."

—Allan Travers

Ty Cobb

Hooks Dauss

## 20 Hooks Dauss

His name may not be the first name to come to mind when thinking of the all-time great Tigers pitchers, but George Dauss holds the record for most wins with 223 and is second in appearances (538) and innings pitched (3,390 2/3). Nicknamed "Hooks" for his wicked curveball, Dauss was a member of the Tigers from 1912 through 1926, winning more than 20 games three times, including a career-high 24 in 1915.

## 21 Special K

The story goes something like this. Back in the 1920s, when Ty Cobb was playing the outfield and also managing the team, he signaled his pitcher, Hooks Dauss, to intentionally walk the great Babe Ruth. Ruth saw the conspicuous signal and waited for the free pass. Dauss reared back and threw a strike right past the unsuspecting Ruth. An apparently angry Cobb threw up his hands and called time. After an animated discussion with his pitcher, Cobb returned to his position and then reacted in disbelief as Dauss threw another pitch right over the plate for strike two. Cobb appeared outraged, called time again, and proceeded to replace not only his pitcher but his catcher, Johnny Bassler, as well. After the obligatory warm-ups, Ruth again took his position in the batter's box, still awaiting his free pass, when Rufe Clarke zipped strike three right past the stunned Ruth, who never took the bat off his shoulder. It's unclear whether the story is truth or legend. Regardless, it still serves as an example of Cobb's ability to outwit anyone in the game.

"EVERY GREAT BATTER WORKS ON THE THEORY THAT THE PITCHER IS MORE AFRAID OF HIM THAN HE IS OF THE PITCHER."

—Ty Cobb

# 22 Wahoo Sam

Despite playing in the shadow of the great Ty Cobb, Sam Crawford, a native of Wahoo, Nebraska, made his own mark as one of the top hitters in the history of baseball. A key member of the great Tigers teams that won three consecutive American League pennants from 1907 to 1909, the right fielder was a lifetime .309 hitter, including a career-high .378 in 1911—the same year Cobb hit .420. Crawford holds the all-time major-league record for triples with 312 and also had 51 inside-the-park home runs. He was inducted into the National Baseball Hall of Fame in 1957.

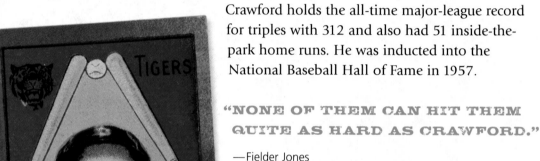

"NONE OF THEM CAN HIT THEM QUITE AS HARD AS CRAWFORD."

—Fielder Jones

# 23 Twice as Nice

Ed "Kickapoo" Summers became the first pitcher in the 20th century to homer twice in one game when he did it while playing for the Tigers in 1910. Summers was an excellent pitcher as well, posting a 24–12 record with a 1.64 ERA in his rookie season of 1908. He threw 18 scoreless innings in a tied game versus the Washington Senators in 1909.

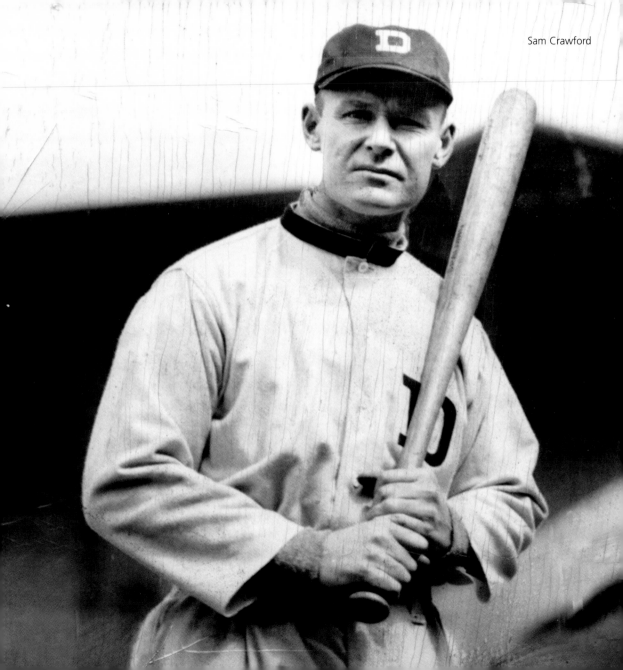

Sam Crawford

Frank Navin and
Mickey Cochrane

# 24 Frank Navin

As a young man, Navin worked in Detroit's gambling houses, and he was a clerk for an insurance firm when his boss, Samuel Angus, purchased the Tigers in 1902. Navin was given the job of bookkeeper and received 10 percent ownership of the club when he brokered a deal between Angus and William Yawkey in 1903. Yawkey had no interest in the day-to-day operations of the club, and Navin took control. He signed Ty Cobb in 1905, brought in manager Hughie Jennings in 1907, and, with co-owner Walter Briggs, made the deal that brought Mickey Cochrane to the Tigers in 1934. Yawkey sold Navin a 50 percent share of the club in 1907, and the two partnered to replace aging Bennett Park with a new stadium in 1911. Yawkey didn't want his name associated with the ballpark, so it became known as Navin Field. Navin guided the Tigers through their early years and desperately wanted to win a world championship for the city of Detroit. He finally got his wish in 1935 — but he died just 37 days later, leaving a legacy that will live forever in Detroit.

# 25 Navin Field/Briggs Stadium

After the close of the 1911 season, Tigers owner Frank Navin had a new 23,000-seat, concrete-and-steel structure built in place of the aging wooden one known as Bennett Park, laying the foundation for what eventually would become Tiger Stadium. Known as Navin Field, the new ballpark featured a 125-foot flagpole within fair territory in center field. Twelve years later, a second deck was added to the grandstand extending from first to third base, expanding seating capacity to 30,000.

When Walter Briggs took over ownership of the team after the death of Navin in 1935, he continued to expand and improve the ballpark, eventually increasing the seating capacity to 53,000. The park was renamed in his honor in 1938.

## 26 Harry Heilmann

The right fielder, who played alongside Ty Cobb, benefited greatly from Cobb's tutelage. In 1921, when Cobb took over as manager of the Tigers, Heilmann's average jumped an incredible 85 points. He led the American League in hitting in 1921, 1923, 1925, and 1927 with averages of .394, .403, .393, and .398, respectively. His .342 career average is third best in major-league history among right-handed hitters and is the second-highest average in Tigers history, behind Cobb's. Heilmann also knocked in more than 100 runs eight times, including a career-high 139 in 1921. After finishing his career in Cincinnati, Heilmann became a broadcaster and spent 17 years in the booth announcing Tigers games. Heilmann was elected to the National Baseball Hall of Fame in 1952.

## 27 Out of This World

The outfield combination of Ty Cobb, Harry Heilmann, and Bobby Veach combined to hit .374 in 1921, with 368 RBI. The team hit .316 for the year, a record that still stands. In 11 full seasons with the Tigers, Veach hit better than .300 eight times, and he led the American League in RBI three times, in 1915, 1917, and 1918.

Left: Bobby Veach
Right: Harry Heilmann

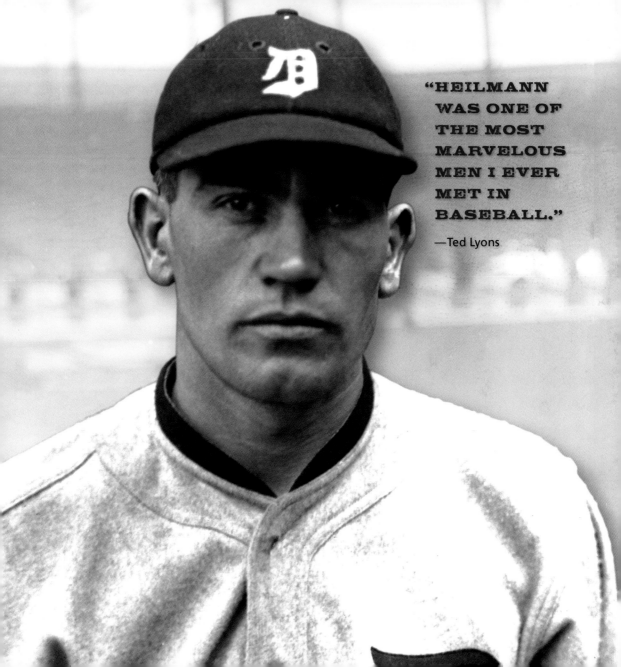

"HEILMANN WAS ONE OF THE MOST MARVELOUS MEN I EVER MET IN BASEBALL."

—Ted Lyons

# 28 More Than a Million

The 1924 Detroit Tigers surpassed one million in attendance, making them the second team in major-league history to reach that milestone. The first? The New York Yankees, of course.

# 29 Fats Fothergill

Bob "Fats" Fothergill was a big man. So big, in fact, that Yankees shortstop Leo Durocher once asked the umpire to declare Fothergill "illegal," reasoning that "both these men can't hit at once." The ploy incensed Fothergill, and he struck out on three pitches. Despite his girth, Fothergill was a terrific hitter. In eight of nine seasons with the Tigers, he hit better than .300, topping .350 four times between 1925 and 1929, and he had a career .327 average as a pinch-hitter. He also was the only player ever to pinch-hit for Ty Cobb, which Fothergill did in 1922. He struck out.

BOB FOTHERGILL  1926
DETROIT TIGERS – OUTFIELD

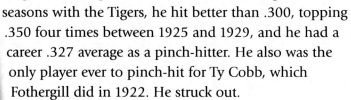

"HE DOES NOT LOOK LIKE A BALL PLAYER, BEING DESIGNED MORE ON THE LINES OF A PROSPEROUS MEAT CUTTER OR ONE USED TO BOOSTING KEGS ON AND OFF A BEER WAGON."

—*Who's Who in Major League Baseball*, 1933, on Fats Fothergill

# 30 Great Names

How could you not like a guy with the name Heinie Manush? In 1926, Manush went 6 for 9 in a doubleheader on the last day of the season to win the American League batting title with a .378 average, besting Babe Ruth by six points. Manush was traded to the St. Louis Browns two years later, played 12 more years, and ended up in the National Baseball Hall of Fame with a lifetime average of .330.

Other former Tigers with great names include Elden Auker, Clyde Barfoot, Skeeter Barnes, Matt Batts, Boom-Boom Beck, Geronimo Berroa, Lu Blue, Flea Clifton, Davey Crockett, Eulogio de la Cruz, Snooks Dowd, Duffy Dyer, Hoot Evers, Happy Finneran, Purnal Goldy, Johnny Hopp, Baby Doll Jacobson, Chick King, Rusty Kuntz, Razor Ledbetter, Slim Love, Firpo Marberry, Bots Nekola, Jimmy Outlaw, Stubby Overmire, Salty Parker, Slicker Parks, Boots Poffenberger, Muddy Ruel, Kid Speer, Lil Stoner, Champ Summers, Coot Veal, Icehouse Wilson, and, of course, Fats Fothergill, Bobo Newsom, Dizzy Trout, Virgil Trucks, and Schoolboy Rowe.

"A HITTING MACHINE, HEINIE MANUSH CONSISTENTLY RANKED AMONG THE GAME'S TOP BATTERS."

—BaseballHallofFame.org

# 31 Hank Greenberg

"Hammerin' Hank" was one of the great power hitters of his generation and possibly the best ever to don the Olde English D. Despite missing the better part of four seasons while serving in the military, and another after suffering a broken wrist, Greenberg hit 306 home runs for the Tigers from 1933 to 1946 and drove in 1,202 runs. The lanky first baseman from The Bronx, New York, endured a torrent of ridicule and racial slurs from fans and other players because of his Jewish heritage. Still, Greenberg remained above it all, winning American League MVP awards in 1935 and 1940 while leading the Tigers to four American League pennants and two World Series titles. He finished with a lifetime batting average of .313, including one year in Pittsburgh, and was inducted into the National Baseball Hall of Fame in 1956. The Tigers retired Greenberg's number, 5, in 1983.

Left: Hank Greenberg is congratulated by teammates after his home run in Game 5 of the 1940 World Series.

"HE WAS ONE OF THE TRULY GREAT HITTERS."

—Joe DiMaggio

## 32 Hank's Grand

After four years of military service, Hank Greenberg returned to the Tigers in July 1945. He homered in his first game back, and slugged a grand slam in the Tigers' final game of the season, keying a 6–3 win over St. Louis as the Tigers won the American League pennant by 1 1/2 games over the Washington Senators.

## 33 Greenberg's Numbers

– Hit .300 or better in eight full seasons, including .348 in 1936
– Totaled 331 home runs for his career, including 58 in 1938, when he fell just two short of tying Babe Ruth's record
– Surpassed 100 RBI seven times, including 183 in 1937, falling just one short of Lou Gehrig's record, and 170 in 1935
– His career slugging percentage of .605 is among the best in baseball history

"I WANTED TO BE KNOWN AS A GREAT BALLPLAYER, PERIOD."

—Hank Greenberg

# 34 The Battalion of Death

The infield lineup of first baseman Hank Greenberg, second baseman Charlie Gehringer, shortstop Billy Rogell, and third baseman Marv Owen set a major-league record in 1934 when they combined to drive in 462 runs. *Detroit Free Press* sportswriter Charles P. Ward christened the quartet "the Battalion of Death."

# 35 The G-Men

Hank Greenberg, Charlie Gehringer, and Goose Goslin formed the triumvirate known as "the G-Men." In 1934, all three players knocked in 100 or more runs and batted better than .300, leading the Tigers to 101 victories and the American League pennant. The following year, the three combined for 387 RBI (Greenberg drove in 170) as the Tigers won their first World Series.

# 36 Schoolboy Rowe

During the pennant-crazed season of 1934, the big man on the mound for the Tigers was Lynwood Thomas "Schoolboy" Rowe. During the year, he tied Walter Johnson's and Lefty Grove's American League record of 16 consecutive victories and finished the season with a 24–8 record. Rowe pitched all 12 innings of a 3–2 win over St. Louis in Game 2 of the 1934 World Series, and he then won 19 games in each of the following two seasons. Arm trouble limited him after that, but he did rebound to go 16–3 in 1940, helping the Tigers to their third AL pennant in seven years.

Mickey Cochrane

# 37 Slip Him a Mickey

When the 1933 season ended, Tigers co-owners Frank Navin and Walter Briggs decided they needed to make a managerial change. Navin wanted to hire the great Babe Ruth, but Ruth was playing hard to get. Briggs was set on getting Mickey Cochrane and put up his own money—$100,000—to sign him. One hardly could argue with the move, as Cochrane led the Tigers to two consecutive pennants, in 1934 and 1935, and their first world championship, in 1935.

# 38 Mickey Cochrane

Cochrane was on the back side of what would become a Hall of Fame career when he was hired as player-manager of the Tigers for the 1934 season. The tough-as-nails catcher also known as "Black Mike" was a natural leader, and he immediately transformed a Tigers team that had won only 75 games in 1933 into a force that cruised to the American League pennant, winning 101 games and finishing seven games in front of the second-place Yankees. Cochrane hit .320 that year and won the AL Most Valuable Player award. He followed up that effort by hitting .319 in 1935, leading his team back to the World Series. Cochrane singled in the ninth and scored the Series-winning run in Game 6, and the Tigers won their first world championship. Cochrane retired as a player in 1937 after suffering a fractured skull when he was hit in the head by a pitch. He returned as manager later that year but was let go by the Tigers in 1938. A lifetime .320 hitter, Cochrane was inducted into the National Baseball Hall of Fame in 1947.

"HOME PLATE WAS HIS, YOU SEE. YOU HAD TO TAKE IT AWAY FROM HIM. TOUGH? JUST THE SAME AS A PIECE OF FLINT."

—Doc Cramer on Mickey Cochrane

# 39 The Golden Goose

When the Tigers brought in clutch-hitting veteran Goose Goslin in 1934, Goslin teamed with fellow "G-Men" Hank Greenberg and Charlie Gehringer to bring Detroit its first pennant since 1909. Then, after the Tigers repeated as American League champions in 1935, Goslin came to the plate in the bottom of the ninth of Game 6 with Mickey Cochrane on second in a 3–3 tie. Goslin lined a single into right field that scored Cochrane, giving Detroit its first World Series title. Goslin was elected to the National Baseball Hall of Fame in 1968.

# 40 Tommy Bridges

With the score tied 3–3 in the top of the ninth inning of Game 6 of the 1935 World Series, Tigers pitcher Tommy Bridges gave up a leadoff triple to Cubs slugger Stan Hack. But Bridges retired the next three batters, stranding Hack at third, and the Tigers won the game and Series in the bottom of the inning. Bridges pitched for the Tigers from 1930 to 1946, tallying 194 wins, including 22 in 1934, 21 in 1935, and 23 in 1936. He also led the league in strikeouts in 1935 and 1936, and was 4–1 in World Series games. Bridges took no-hitters into the ninth inning four times, but never was able to complete the gem. His 33 shutouts rank third all-time in Tigers history.

Left to right: Schoolboy Rowe, Mickey Cochrane, Elden Auker, Tommy Bridges, and Alvin Crowder

Mickey Cochrane scores
the winning run in Game
6 of the 1935 World Series.

# 41 Finally!

After a bitter ending to the thrilling 1934 season, the Tigers started slowly in 1935 and were mired in last place early in the season. But behind the slugging of Hank Greenberg and a solid pitching staff, Detroit rebounded to win its second straight pennant and returned to the World Series, this time to face a familiar foe: the Chicago Cubs. The Cubs came in with loads of confidence, having won 21 straight games in September, and Chicago ace Lon Warneke didn't disappoint Cubs fans, shutting out the Tigers, 3–0, in Game 1. Hank Greenberg homered in a four-run first inning in Game 2, but later broke his wrist trying to score from first base and missed the rest of the Series. Given Detroit's past failures in the Series, the devastating injury could have dealt a mortal blow to the team's hopes, but the Tigers persevered and won Game 2, 8–3. They followed that with a dramatic 6–5, 11-inning victory in Game 3 on Jo-Jo White's run-scoring single, and a 2–1 win in Game 4, to take a 3-games-to-1 lead in the Series. The Tigers had a chance to close out the Series in Game 5, but Warneke again shut them down, earning a 3–1 win. Game 6 was a tense battle that went to the bottom of the ninth with the game tied at 3 apiece. With two outs, Goose Goslin lined a single that scored Mickey Cochrane from second, and the Detroit Tigers won the World Series for the first time. Delirious fans poured onto Navin Field and then spilled out into the streets. The entire city of Detroit went crazy, celebrating all night long. It was the perfect tonic for the Depression-weary town that had been waiting decades for this moment. Finally, it had arrived.

## "I WAITED 30 YEARS FOR THIS DAY. I CAN NOW DIE IN PEACE."

—Frank Navin

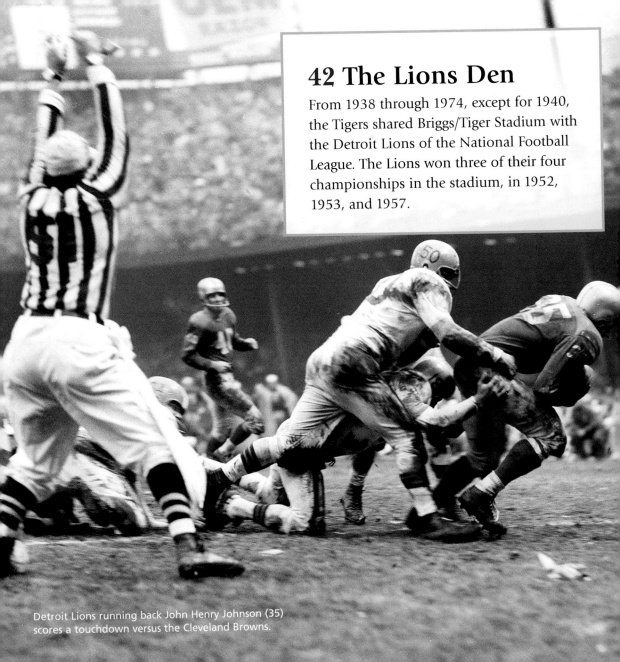

## 42 The Lions Den

From 1938 through 1974, except for 1940, the Tigers shared Briggs/Tiger Stadium with the Detroit Lions of the National Football League. The Lions won three of their four championships in the stadium, in 1952, 1953, and 1957.

Detroit Lions running back John Henry Johnson (35) scores a touchdown versus the Cleveland Browns.

# 43 City of Champions

Detroit became known as "the City of Champions" in 1935–36. After the Tigers broke through and won the World Series in the fall of 1935, the Detroit Lions followed by winning their first National Football League championship just a couple of months later. Then the Detroit Red Wings of the National Hockey League kept the streak going by winning their first Stanley Cup at the conclusion of the 1935–36 season, to cap an incredible run by Motor City teams.

# 44 Walter Briggs

Legend has it that in 1907, Walter Briggs, a regular-season box-seats holder, was incensed when he learned he would not be able to purchase those same seats for the World Series. Briggs insisted on a face-to-face meeting with owner Frank Navin. He came away with his tickets and vowed someday to purchase the team himself. After William Yawkey died in 1919, Briggs, who had made his fortune in the automobile industry, and John Kelsey each purchased a quarter share of the Tigers and became partners with Frank Navin. Briggs, who bought Kelsey's share in 1927, essentially was a silent partner and let Navin run the club, but he was invested totally in the success of the ball club and plowed all his profits back into the team and ballpark. With Navin, he was responsible for the continuing improvement and expansion of the stadium, and when he took over complete ownership of the club after Navin's death in 1937, he added a second deck to the left- and center-field stands, expanding the stadium's seating capacity to 53,000. He also changed the name from Navin Field to Briggs Stadium. Although he was one of the last owners to install lights in his ballpark and waited much too long to integrate the club, Briggs was completely devoted to his team. His contributions to the Tigers, the city of Detroit, and the game of baseball were exceptional.

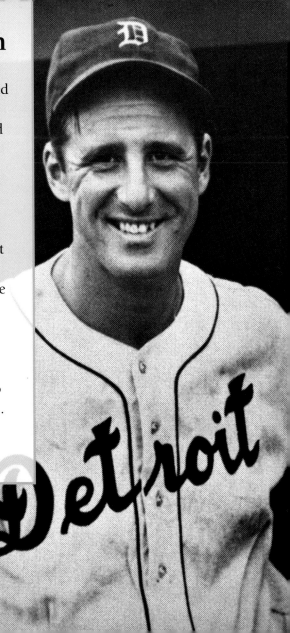

# 45 The Mechanical Man

Many consider Charlie Gehringer to be the best second baseman of all time. Nicknamed "the Mechanical Man" by Lefty Gomez for his incredible consistency, Gehringer posted a batting average of .300 or better 13 times, winning the American League MVP award and batting title in 1937 with an average of .371. The smooth-swinging lefty hit .320 for his career while driving in 1,427 runs, topping the 100-RBI mark in seven different seasons. Mentored by Ty Cobb when he came up in 1924, Gehringer spent his entire career with the Tigers, remaining with the club until 1942 when he was called into military service. Quiet and unassuming, Gehringer was the ultimate team player on some great Tigers squads. He was elected to the National Baseball Hall of Fame in 1949. His number, 2, was retired by the Tigers in 1983.

"GEHRINGER WAS MAGIC. GREAT BAT, GRACEFUL FIELDER, CONSUMMATE TEAM MAN."

—Lynn Henning, from the *Detroit News*

Hank Greenberg and Charlie Gehringer

—Rudy York

Rudy York trots home after one of his record 18 home runs in August 1937.

# 46 Rudy York

York was the classic designated hitter long before there was such a thing. No great shakes in the field, he was moved from position to position so the Tigers could keep his powerful bat in the lineup. He was so good at the plate, the Tigers eventually moved future Hall of Famer Hank Greenberg to the outfield so they could use York at first base. In his nine-plus seasons with the Tigers, York hit 239 home runs, including a career-high 35 in his rookie season of 1937. Incredibly, York hit 18 of those 35 homers in August, setting a major-league record that lasted until 1998, when it was broken by Sammy Sosa.

# 47 How 'bout That Feller?

The expectations weren't high for the Tigers in 1940 after they had finished a distant 26 1/2 games behind the New York Yankees the previous year. But with Hank Greenberg smacking 41 homers and driving in 150 runs, and second-year outfielder Barney McCosky hitting .340, the Tigers surprisingly found themselves in a showdown with the Cleveland Indians to determine the pennant in the last week of the season. Not wanting to sacrifice either of his best pitchers, Schoolboy Rowe or Bobo Newsom, in a head-to-head matchup with Indians ace Bob Feller in the first of the three-game set, Tigers manager Del Baker countered with late-season call-up Floyd Giebell. Feller held the Tigers to three hits, but Rudy York's two-run homer proved to be the difference as the surprising Giebell shut out the Indians on six hits. It was the last game he won in the major leagues. The pennant belonged to the Tigers, and they went on to face Cincinnati in the World Series.

Dizzy Trout

# 48 Bobo

He called himself Bobo. And he called virtually everyone else Bobo as well. Louis "Bobo" Newsom's major-league career spanned 25 years, from 1929 to 1953, and he played for nine franchises. He came to Detroit in 1939, and in 1940 he helped lead the Tigers to the World Series, winning a career-high 21 games. Newsom got the start in Game 1 of the World Series and shut down the Cincinnati bats in a 7–2 Tigers win. His father, who had traveled to Cincinnati to watch his son pitch, died of a heart attack early the next morning. The heartbroken Newsom buried his father, then returned to pitch in Game 5, throwing a three-hit shutout to give the Tigers a 3-games-to-2 lead in the Series. Newsom returned to the mound on a single day's rest to pitch Game 7, but he and the Tigers succumbed to the Reds 2–1 in the finale, bringing a sad conclusion to an unforgettable season.

# 49 Dizzy Trout

His name alone deserves mentioning, but Paul "Dizzy" Trout's accomplishments earned him a place in Tigers lore as well. In 14 seasons with the Tigers, Trout won 161 games. After winning 20 games in 1943, he went 27–14 in 1944 with 33 complete games and a league-leading ERA of 2.12, pitching a staggering 352 1/3 innings. In the championship year of 1945, Trout won 18 more games, winning four times in eight days during the heat of the September pennant race. He threw a complete-game five-hitter in Game 4 of the World Series, defeating the Cubs 4–1.

"OL' DIZ LIKES THE LIMELIGHT."

—Paul Richards

# 50 A Familiar Foe

The Tigers faced a familiar foe, the Chicago Cubs, in the 1945 World Series. It marked the fourth time in seven visits to the Fall Classic that the Tigers squared off against the Cubs. The 1945 World Series generally is regarded as one of the worst-played Series in history. World War II had taken its toll on the rosters of every major-league team, and the quality of play suffered for it. But with Hank Greenberg back in the lineup and Hal Newhouser leading the way on the mound, the Tigers bested the Cubs 4 games to 3 for their second world championship. Newhouser got bombed in a 9–0 Game 1 loss, but he rebounded to win Game 5 and give Detroit a 3-games-to-2 lead. The Tigers rallied from a 7–3 deficit in Game 6 to tie the game on an eighth-inning homer by Greenberg, but Chicago prevailed in 12 innings for an 8–7 victory, sending the Series to Game 7. Newhouser came up big in the finale, going the distance and striking out 10 in a 9–3 Tigers win, bringing a second world championship to Detroit.

Hal Newhouser, left and inset, broadcaster
Ty Tyson, and Steve O'Neill

# 51 Prince Hal

Hal Newhouser was a schoolboy star in Detroit and turned down a much more lucrative offer from the Cleveland Indians to play for his hometown team. "Prince Hal" joined the Tigers in 1939, at the age of 18, and gradually developed into one of the premier pitchers of his time. From 1944 through 1946, Newhouser was 80–27, winning 29, 25, and 26 games, respectively. He was named American League MVP in 1944 and 1945—the only pitcher ever to be awarded consecutive MVPs—and led his team to a World Series title in 1945, winning Games 5 and 7.

Newhouser, who remained with the Tigers through 1953, ranks fourth on Detroit's all-time list with 200 wins. His 1,770 strikeouts are third best, he's tied for third in shutouts with 33, and he is fourth all-time with 212 complete games. Newhouser was elected to the National Baseball Hall of Fame in 1992, and his number, 16, was retired by the Tigers in 1997.

"NEWHOUSER...
HAD ALL THE
PITCHES."

—Lynn Henning,
from the *Detroit News*

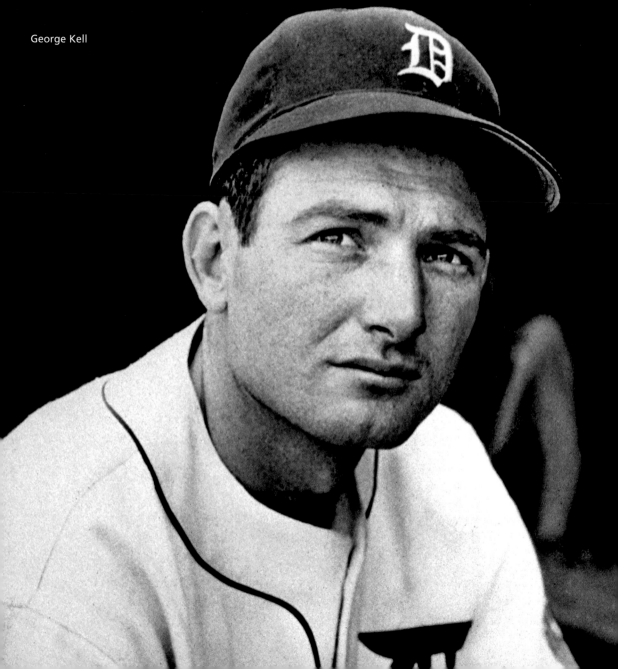
George Kell

# 52 George Kell

The Tigers received third baseman George Kell from the Philadelphia Athletics for outfielder Barney McCosky in a 1946 trade that stunned much of the baseball world. From 1946 to 1951, Kell never hit lower than .304. He hit a career-high and league-leading .343 in 1949 and followed that with a .340 average and a career-high 101 RBI in 1950. A tireless worker, Kell made a study of hitting, often altering his stance depending on the situation and what pitch he was expecting. He also was a terrific third baseman and was considered to be one of the best of his era.

In 1949, Kell nipped the Red Sox' Ted Williams by the slimmest of margins for the American League batting title. Kell went 2 for 3 on the final day, while Williams was 0 for 2 with two walks, giving Kell the title with an average of .3429 to Williams' .3427. Kell was traded to the Red Sox during the 1952 season in a nine-player swap that brought Johnny Pesky and Walt Dropo to the Tigers. Kell played for several more years before retiring in 1957. He was elected to the National Baseball Hall of Fame in 1983.

After his retirement as a player, Kell joined the Tigers broadcast team in 1959, first as a radio commentator, then moving to television. With a smooth southern drawl and a natural, down-to-earth style, Kell provided a warm and honest account of the action. Fans fell in love with him all over again as "the voice of the Tigers," and he treated them to nearly four decades of Tigers baseball from his place in the broadcast booth.

"DETROIT WAS THE PERFECT PLACE FOR ME TO PLAY."

—George Kell, from *The Detroit Tigers Encyclopedia*

# 53 The Voices

In additon to former Tiger greats Harry Heilmann, George Kell, and Al Kaline, who successfully made the transition from the field to the broadcast booth, Ty Tyson and Ernie Harwell earned a place in Tigers history as beloved broadcasters. Tyson was the original voice of the Tigers, hired in 1927, and he remained in the booth through 1942. He returned to try his hand at television in 1947, before retiring for good in 1952.

Ernie Harwell joined George Kell in the Tigers broadcast booth in 1960. His low-key delivery was popular with fans in the blue-collar town, and Harwell became a legend in Detroit. When his contract wasn't renewed in 1992, fans were outraged, threatening to boycott games. He was rehired later that year. Harwell remained with the Tigers until his retirement after the 2002 season. He received the Ford C. Frick Award for broadcasting from the National Baseball Hall of Fame in 1981, and the Tigers placed a statue of Harwell in front of Comerica Park in his honor.

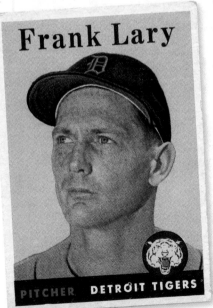

# 54 The Yankee Killer

From 1947 through 1964, the New York Yankees appeared in 15 World Series, winning 10. It was the height of their dynasty. But for a two-year stretch during that incredible run, from August 26, 1957, to August 4, 1959, Tigers pitcher Frank Lary was nearly unbeatable when facing the Yanks, posting a 13–1 record.

"ME BEING A SOUTHERN BOY, I NEVER THOUGHT YANKEES WAS TOO SMART."

—Frank Lary, from the *Detroit News*

"THAT BALL IS LOOOOOOONG GONE!"
—Ernie Harwell

Virgil Trucks after his
second no-hitter in 1952

## 55 Trucks' Stops

Back in 1952, Virgil Trucks threw not one but two no-hitters for the Tigers in the same season. His first came May 15, when he shut down the Washington Senators, getting the 1–0 win on a two-out, ninth-inning homer by Vic Wertz. Three months later, on August 25, Trucks repeated the feat, this time against the mighty Yankees, again winning 1–0. Only three other pitchers—Johnny Vander Meer, Allie Reynolds, and Nolan Ryan—have pitched two no-hitters in the same year. And by the way, Trucks finished the 1952 season with a record of 5–19 and was traded to the St. Louis Browns.

## 56 Jim Bunning

A lot of folks remember Jim Bunning for the perfect game he threw for the Philadelphia Phillies in 1964 versus the New York Mets, but Bunning actually was a terrific pitcher for the Tigers for nine years before being traded to the Phillies after the 1963 season. Bunning won 118 games for the Tigers from 1955 to 1963, including his only 20-win season, in 1957, when he went 20–8 with an ERA of 2.69. He threw a no-hitter against Boston in 1958, and he led the AL in strikeouts in 1959 and 1960 with 201 each year. Bunning went on to finish his career with 224 wins, making him the first pitcher since Cy Young to win more than 100 games in each league. He was elected to the National Baseball Hall of Fame in 1996 and currently is a member of the U.S. Senate representing the state of Kentucky.

Jim Bunning

PITCHER  DETROIT TIGERS

# 57 Tiger Stadium

The Tigers had been playing baseball at "The Corner" since 1896, but it wasn't until 1961, when ownership of the team passed to John Fetzer, that the ballpark finally was renamed Tiger Stadium. So many memories are forever etched in the old park, which opened in 1912 as Navin Field. So many patrons passed through its gates, spending glorious afternoons and unforgettable evenings. As the world passed by outside, decade after decade, inside the Tigers stayed true to their hometown, playing their blue-collar style of baseball, and delivering two more World Series titles, in 1968 and 1984. When Todd Jones struck out Kansas City's Carlos Beltran to close out an 8–2 Tigers win in the home finale of the 1999 season, the grand old ballpark had hosted its last Tigers game. A moving postgame celebration was held, and longtime Tigers broadcasting legend Ernie Harwell said a final farewell to the venerable home of the Tigers.

Tiger Stadium, 1999

# 58 His Sunday Best

Charlie "Paw Paw" Maxwell had a knack for hitting home runs on Sunday. Of the 148 round-trippers Maxwell hit during his career, 40 came on Sunday. The Tigers outfielder who lived in Paw Paw, Michigan, hit a career-high 31 in 1959, homering in four straight at bats in a May 3 doubleheader—on a Sunday, naturally.

# 59 John Fetzer

Fetzer was a part of a group that purchased the Tigers from the Briggs family in 1956. He bought out his partners and by 1961 owned the team outright. A multimillionaire who had made his fortune in radio and television, Fetzer loved the Tigers and served as their guardian for more than 20 years. He became one of the most powerful and influential owners in baseball, and he did his best to make decisions that helped the game and not just his team. In an effort to reconnect the team with the community, Fetzer renamed the ballpark Tiger Stadium. He promoted Jim Campbell to general manager, where he remained until 1992, and Fetzer negotiated the first national television contract for the major leagues, which created the revenue stream that has helped finance Major League Baseball ever since. A quiet, conservative man of utmost integrity, Fetzer and his right-hand man Campbell were rewarded for their efforts with a world championship in 1968. When Fetzer sold the Tigers to Tom Monaghan at the conclusion of the 1983 season, he handed over a team that would win the World Series the following year.

"I HAVE NEVER CONSIDERED MYSELF THE OWNER OF THE TIGERS. I SERVE MERELY AS THE CLUB'S GUARDIAN. THE TIGERS BELONG TO THE FANS."

—John Fetzer

John Fetzer
and manager
Mayo Smith

# 60 Al Kaline

The Tigers signed the shy, skinny kid from Baltimore out of high school, and Kaline went straight to the majors, never spending a day in the minor leagues. In 1955, in Kaline's second full season with the Tigers, he hit .340 and won the AL batting title, making him the youngest ever to lead the league in hitting; he broke former Tigers great Ty Cobb's record by a single day. Known as "Mr. Tiger," Kaline spent 22 years in Detroit, patrolling right field and compiling a career batting average of .297. He is the all-time leader or near the top in several Tigers statistical categories. After he retired in 1975, Kaline joined George Kell in the broadcast booth, spending more than 25 years there before accepting a position in the Tigers' front office. His number, 6, was the first to be retired by the Tigers, in 1980. Kaline was a first-ballot inductee into the National Baseball Hall of Fame that same year.

"THE FELLA WHO COULD DO EVERYTHING IS AL KALINE. HE WAS JUST THE EPITOME OF WHAT A GREAT OUTFIELDER IS ALL ABOUT."
—Brooks Robinson

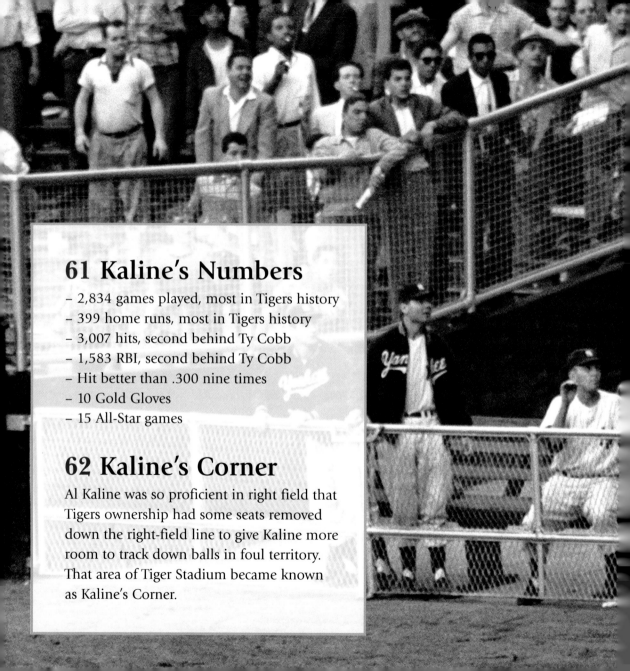

## 61 Kaline's Numbers

- 2,834 games played, most in Tigers history
- 399 home runs, most in Tigers history
- 3,007 hits, second behind Ty Cobb
- 1,583 RBI, second behind Ty Cobb
- Hit better than .300 nine times
- 10 Gold Gloves
- 15 All-Star games

## 62 Kaline's Corner

Al Kaline was so proficient in right field that
Tigers ownership had some seats removed
down the right-field line to give Kaline more
room to track down balls in foul territory.
That area of Tiger Stadium became known
as Kaline's Corner.

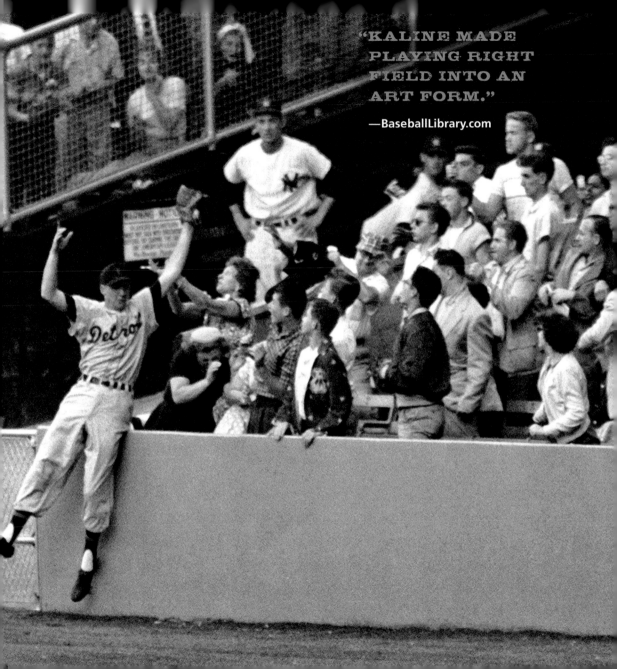

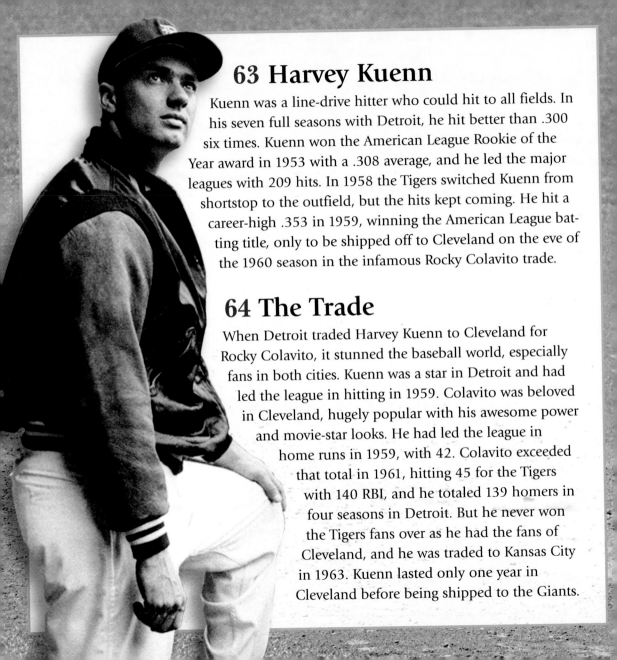

## 63 Harvey Kuenn

Kuenn was a line-drive hitter who could hit to all fields. In his seven full seasons with Detroit, he hit better than .300 six times. Kuenn won the American League Rookie of the Year award in 1953 with a .308 average, and he led the major leagues with 209 hits. In 1958 the Tigers switched Kuenn from shortstop to the outfield, but the hits kept coming. He hit a career-high .353 in 1959, winning the American League batting title, only to be shipped off to Cleveland on the eve of the 1960 season in the infamous Rocky Colavito trade.

## 64 The Trade

When Detroit traded Harvey Kuenn to Cleveland for Rocky Colavito, it stunned the baseball world, especially fans in both cities. Kuenn was a star in Detroit and had led the league in hitting in 1959. Colavito was beloved in Cleveland, hugely popular with his awesome power and movie-star looks. He had led the league in home runs in 1959, with 42. Colavito exceeded that total in 1961, hitting 45 for the Tigers with 140 RBI, and he totaled 139 homers in four seasons in Detroit. But he never won the Tigers fans over as he had the fans of Cleveland, and he was traded to Kansas City in 1963. Kuenn lasted only one year in Cleveland before being shipped to the Giants.

# 65 DeWitt's Wisdom?

In 1960, Tigers general manager Bill DeWitt sent skipper Jimmy Dykes to the Cleveland Indians for manager Joe Gordon in a one-of-a-kind manager-for-manager trade. Gordon quit in frustration at the end of the year. To his credit, DeWitt already had completed trades for Norm Cash and Rocky Colavito before making the Dykes-for-Gordon deal.

Above: Harvey Kuenn
Left: Rocky Colavito

# 66 Stormin' Norman

Few have ever played the game harder than Norm Cash or enjoyed it more. Cash played with an intensity and unbridled enthusiasm that was infectious, and he became an all-time favorite in Detroit. Acquired from the Indians for Steve Demeter just before the start of the 1960 season, Cash was a classic left-handed power hitter. In just his second season with the Tigers, in 1961, the slugging first baseman homered 41 times and drove in 132 runs, while batting a league-best .361. All three marks were career highs. That same year, he became the first Tiger ever to knock a ball completely out of Tiger Stadium, clearing the right-field roof on June 11. Cash's 373 home runs are second to Al Kaline's 399 on the Tigers' all-time list. He also was a prodigious strikeout king, fanning 1,081 times in 15 seasons with the Tigers, second only to Lou Whitaker.

# 67 Trying to Get a Leg Up

On July 15, 1973, future Hall of Famer Nolan Ryan was on the verge of throwing the second no-hitter of his career when Norm Cash strolled to the plate with two outs in the bottom of the ninth. Cash already was 0 for 3, striking out in each at bat. Figuring he couldn't do much worse against the flame-throwing Ryan, Cash brought a table leg with him instead of his bat. Umpire Ron Luciano wouldn't allow Cash to hit with the nonconforming piece of equipment, so Cash returned to the dugout and came back with his regular bat, only to strike out for the fourth time.

Norm Cash

Gates Brown
taking batting
practice while
Jack Pierce
looks on

## 68 The Gator

William "Gates" Brown didn't play every day. His career batting average was a modest .257. And yet "the Gator" was one of the most beloved Tigers of all time. After serving a year in prison for burglary, Brown was signed by the Tigers in 1959, and homered in his first major-league at bat, in 1963. He was the quintessential pinch-hitter, time and again coming off the bench to deliver a clutch hit. Brown was instrumental in the Tigers' run to a third world championship in 1968, when he hit .370. He remained a major contributor until his retirement in 1975.

## 69 Mustard with That?

Once, after Jim Northrup had gotten himself and Gates Brown a hot dog while sitting on the dugout bench, Brown was called on to pinch-hit before he'd had a chance to enjoy his tasty snack. Unwilling to leave it with Northrup, Brown stuffed the mustard-slathered frankfurter into his jersey and trotted out to the batter's box. He then lined a shot into the gap in right field, which he stretched into a double with a head-first slide into second. When Brown stood up, he had a huge yellow smear across the front of his uniform—a Tiger stripe, if you will.

# 70 Denny McLain

McLain's story is both a fairy tale and a cautionary tale. The right-hander debuted with the Tigers in 1963, and in 1966 he won 20 games, showing flashes of the pitching brilliance that was to come. After winning 17 games in 1967, McLain had a year that never will be forgotten, in 1968. He won 31 games, losing only 6, while striking out 280 and posting an ERA of 1.96. It was one of the most dominant pitching performances in the history of major-league baseball—no one had won 30 games since Dizzy Dean in 1934. McLain won both the AL Cy Young and MVP awards, and the Tigers captured their third World Series title. He followed up his historic year with a 24–9 season, but 1970 brought all kinds of trouble— McLain was suspended three different times—and the Tigers traded him to the Washington Senators. Not yet 30 years old, McLain was out of baseball in 1973 and eventually wound up serving two prison terms on various drug, embezzlement, and racketeering charges.

# 71 The Music Man

After the 1968 season, Denny McLain, an accomplished organ player, recorded a couple of albums for Capitol Records: *Denny McLain at the Organ: The Detroit Tigers Superstar Swings with Today's Hits* and *Denny McLain in Las Vegas.*

"I FELT ABSOLUTELY INVINCIBLE THAT YEAR."

—Denny McLain on 1968, from the *Detroit News*

# 72 1968

After falling one game short of the AL pennant in 1967 with a loss on the final day of the season, the Tigers began 1968 with absolute determination to avoid another bitter disappointment. Following an opening day loss, Detroit reeled off nine straight wins and was off and running. A 11-game winning streak late in the season sealed the pennant, as the Tigers won a team-record 103 games (broken in 1984) and finished 12 games in front of second-place Baltimore. Denny McLain's 31 wins headlined the effort, and the Tigers moved on to face the St. Louis Cardinals in the World Series.

Game 1 featured a classic matchup between the best starting pitchers from both leagues—McLain versus Bob Gibson. Gibson dominated, striking out a World Series–record 17 hitters, and St. Louis won, 4–0. Mickey Lolich pitched the Tigers to a Game 2 win, but St. Louis took Game 3, and Gibson was once again dominant in a 10–1 Cardinals victory in Game 4. The Series turned when Willie Horton threw out Lou Brock at the plate in the fifth inning of Game 5 and the Tigers rallied for a 5–3 win. McLain pitched his best game of the Series in Game 6 and the Tigers battered the Cards 13–1, setting up a Game 7 showdown. Gibson was once again on the mound for St. Louis, opposed by Lolich. Both pitchers held the opposition scoreless through six innings, but the Tigers broke through for three runs in the top of the seventh on four consecutive two-out hits, highlighted by Jim Northrup's two-run triple. When Lolich induced Tim McCarver to pop out to Bill Freehan in the bottom of the ninth, the Tigers had won their third World Series.

Willie Horton homers off Nelson Briles in Game 2 of the 1968 World Series.

Jim Northrup's grand slam, Game 6, 1968

# 73 Mayo's Move

As the 1968 World Series approached, manager Mayo Smith had a significant problem to address—how to get four outfielders in three positions. Earlier in the season, when Al Kaline had gone down with an injury, Jim Northrup had filled in spectacularly. But with Kaline back in the lineup, Smith had no place to put Northrup, with stars Willie Horton and Mickey Stanley in left and center fields. Smith knew that Stanley regularly took infield practice as part of his training regimen, and he decided to move Stanley to shortstop, replacing the light-hitting Ray Oyler. This allowed Smith to put Northrup in center field and get all four bats in the lineup. It was an extremely risky move, considering Stanley had never played shortstop in the majors, but it paid off. Stanley was solid and Northrup homered twice and drove in eight runs in the Series, including a grand slam in Game 6. In the end, Smith's highly questioned move proved to be a stroke of genius.

# 74 So Grand

Jim Northrup spent 10 years in a Tigers uniform, but his 1968 season featured enough highlights to fill a career. Sharing time in the outfield with Willie Horton, Mickey Stanley, and Al Kaline, who missed several weeks with a shoulder injury, Northrup led the team in hits (153) and RBI (90). He hit three grand slams in one week, including going back-to-back on June 24 versus Cleveland. His grand slam off the Cardinals' Larry Jaster in the 10-run third inning of Game 6 of the World Series keyed that win, and his two-run triple off Bob Gibson in the seventh inning of Game 7 scored the Series-clinching run for the Tigers.

"THEY RAISED ME. ALL
I KNOW IS THE TIGERS."

—Willie Horton, from the *Detroit News*

# 75 Willie Horton

Horton grew up in Detroit, and was a Tiger through and through. The youngest of 21 children, Horton signed with the Tigers right out of high school, and he came up to the big leagues in September 1963. In his first full season with the Tigers, in 1965, Horton hammered 29 home runs and had 104 RBI. He followed that with 27 homers and 100 RBI in 1966. But his best season may have been in the championship year of 1968. He smacked a career-high 36 round-trippers and made the play that turned the World Series, when he threw out Lou Brock at the plate during Game 5. For his career, Horton hit 325 home runs, 262 with the Tigers, ranking him fourth all-time with Detroit. Like many baseball players, Horton was superstitious. So superstitious, in fact, that he used the same batting helmet his entire career, repainting it when he changed teams. Forever beloved by Tigers fans, Horton saw his number, 23, retired by the team in 2000, and a statue commemorating his achievements stands in Comerica Park, alongside one of Hall of Famer Ty Cobb.

Bill Freehan tags out Lou Brock in Game 5 of the 1968 World Series.

## 76 The Play

It ranks as one of the great plays in World Series history and clearly changed the course of the 1968 Series. With St. Louis leading 3–2 in Game 5 and already up 3 games to 1 in the Series, Lou Brock stood on second in the top of the fifth. With one out, Julian Javier lined a Mickey Lolich pitch into left field for a base hit. Brock had every intention of scoring on the play and motored around third toward home. Willie Horton fielded the ball and came up throwing. He fired a strike to catcher Bill Freehan, who blocked Brock's path to the plate. Brock came in standing up instead of sliding under Freehan's tag, and Freehan held his ground. As the two players collided, Freehan tagged Brock out, and the Cardinals didn't score again the rest of the game. The Tigers plated three runs in the seventh and won the game 5–3.

## 77 Bill Freehan

Freehan probably is remembered best for both catching Tim McCarver's foul pop that ended the 1968 World Series and for tagging Lou Brock at the plate during Game 5, which turned the tide of the Series. But it was Freehan's solid, steady presence behind the plate that made him one of the best catchers of his era. After a brief call-up in 1961, Freehan became a regular in 1963 and hit a career-high .300 in 1964, in just his second full season in the big leagues. His performance earned him the first of 10 consecutive All-Star Game appearances (11 overall).

Freehan had career highs of 25 home runs and 84 RBI in the championship year of 1968, and he finished his career with 200 home runs and 758 runs batted in. An outstanding defensive catcher as well, Freehan won five consecutive Gold Gloves from 1965 to 1969, and he set major-league records for putouts, total chances, and highest fielding percentage as the longtime Tigers backstop.

# 78 Mickey Lolich

Lolich was a portly, motorcycle-riding free spirit who hardly fit the description of a successful major-league pitcher. But the man could throw strikes, and he became one of the best, most consistent pitchers in Tigers history. From 1964 to 1974, Lolich never won fewer than 14 games, recording more than 200 strikeouts seven times. His performance in the 1968 World Series is legendary. Playing second fiddle to 31-game winner Denny McLain, Lolich upstaged his teammate by winning three games in the Series, including a Game 7 4–1 win over Hall of Famer Bob Gibson on just two days' rest. In those three complete games, Lolich recorded 21 strikeouts and an ERA of 1.67. He also batted .250 with a home run and two RBI. A workhorse, Lolich had his best season in 1971, posting a 25–14 record with 308 strikeouts and a 2.92 ERA while pitching an incredible 376 innings. He followed that with a 22–14 record in 1972, with 250 strikeouts and an ERA of 2.50. Lolich is the Tigers' all-time leader in strikeouts (2,679), starts (459), and shutouts (39). He's third in wins with 207 and one of only four Tigers pitchers ever to throw more than 3,000 innings. Not bad for a self-proclaimed "fat guy."

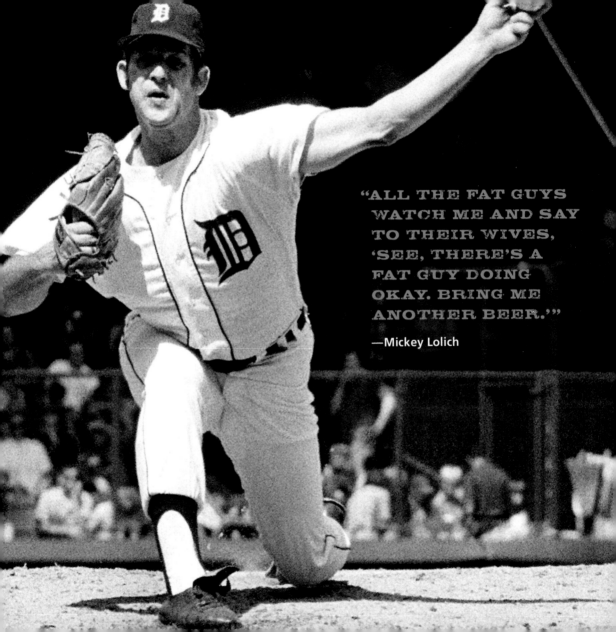

"ALL THE FAT GUYS WATCH ME AND SAY TO THEIR WIVES, 'SEE, THERE'S A FAT GUY DOING OKAY. BRING ME ANOTHER BEER.'"

—Mickey Lolich

COULDN'T BE OVER,
BECAUSE I COULDN'T
DO ANYTHING ELSE."

—John Hiller, from the *Detroit News*

# 79 The Comeback

John Hiller was a so-so pitcher for the Tigers from 1965 through 1970, never winning more than nine games in a season. But after suffering a heart attack prior to the start of the 1971 season and undergoing intestinal bypass surgery, Hiller worked himself back into shape and returned to the Tigers in the summer of 1972, helping Detroit secure the AL East Division title by one-half game over Boston, posting an ERA of 2.03 in 24 appearances and recording three saves. Then, in 1973, he had a season to remember, going 10–5 with an ERA of 1.44 while saving a team-record 38 games. After his heart attack, doctors had thought Hiller might never pitch again, but his performance in 1973 earned him the Comeback Player of the Year award. Hiller won a career-high 17 games in 1974 and continued to pitch for the Tigers until he retired in 1980.

# 80 One in a Million

Ron LeFlore started playing baseball while serving a sentence for armed robbery in Jackson State Prison. In 1973, when Tigers manager Billy Martin made a goodwill visit to the prison, he saw LeFlore play and offered him a tryout when he was released. Out on a weekend furlough, LeFlore called the Tigers and was given an informal tryout. Impressed with his speed and natural abilities, the Tigers signed LeFlore after he was paroled, and LeFlore got the call up to the majors the next year. He hit .300 or better three of four years from 1976 to 1979, led the league in stolen bases with 68 in 1978, and stole 78 more the following year, before he was traded to the Montreal Expos following the 1979 season. His story was made into a movie, appropriately titled *One in a Million*.

# 81 The Bird

In major-league baseball, 1976 was the year of "the Bird." Mark Fidrych, a 21-year-old who out of uniform looked like your everyday student in his faded jeans and worn-out sneakers, took the baseball world by storm. Given the nickname "the Bird" because this tall, lanky kid with a loose gait and floppy hair reminded a coach of Big Bird on *Sesame Street*, Fidrych possessed a rare talent when on the mound, and America quickly found out just how good he was. The Bird made the team out of spring training and spent his first five weeks in the bullpen. He finally was called on to start on May 15, and the frenzy began. Fidrych went 19–9, completing 24 of 29 starts, and led the league with an ERA of 2.34. He was chosen as the starting pitcher for the American League in the All-Star Game.

The Bird was a sensation. Fans flocked to see him. Whether at home in Tiger Stadium or on the road, attendance always was dramatically higher when Fidrych was pitching. The kid stooped to smooth the dirt on the mound with his hands. He walked around between pitches, constantly talking to himself and the balls, telling them where to go before he threw them. Folks couldn't get enough of him. He was asked to appear on numerous television shows. He met famous actors and rock stars. A Michigan legislator even suggested that Fidrych be made the official state bird. But it all came to an end much too quickly. Fidrych tore cartilage in his knee in spring training the following year and missed the first two months of the season. After winning six of his first eight starts when he returned, Fidrych suffered a torn rotator cuff in his throwing shoulder and never was the same again. He won only four more games and pitched his last major-league game in 1980. But for one year, 1976, Fidrych was flying high.

"THE WHOLE SEASON WAS LIKE ONE GIANT TRIP."

—Mark Fidrych, from *The Detroit Tigers Encyclopedia*

Mark Fidrych

# 82 Alan Trammell

Smart, consistent, reliable, a natural leader—all these describe Trammell, and yet he was so much more. The steady shortstop spent 20 years in Detroit and earned a spot among the most respected and beloved Tigers of all time. Seven times Trammell hit .300 or better, and in 1987, when manager Sparky Anderson asked his shortstop to bat cleanup, Trammell delivered with his best offensive year ever, batting .343 with 28 home runs and 105 RBI—all career highs. He won four Gold Gloves and played in six All-Star games. Trammell hit .450 in the 1984 World Series, driving in six runs and winning the Series MVP award. He accounted for all four runs in the Tigers' Game 4 win, with two two-run home runs. In 2003, Trammell was named manager of the Tigers, but he was let go after the 2005 season.

"I'LL ALWAYS BE A TIGER."

—Alan Trammell

# 83 Sweet Lou

"Sweet Lou" Whitaker was considered one of the most gifted all-around athletes ever to play for the Tigers. Whitaker possessed incredible range at second base, a cannon for an arm, and terrific speed on the base paths. Over time he also developed some pop in his bat, hitting 20 or more home runs four times. Whitaker was a five-time All-Star, won three Gold Glove awards, and was named 1978 AL Rookie of the Year. At the 1983 All-Star Game in Chicago, Whitaker's uniform didn't make it to the ballpark with him, and he played the game in a souvenir jersey with his number, 1, drawn on the back in black marker. He is one of only two second basemen, with Joe Morgan, to play 2,000 games, get 2,000 hits, and smack 200 home runs. Sweet, Lou.

# 84 A Perfect Combo

Shortstop Alan Trammell and second baseman Lou Whitaker made their major-league debuts the same year, 1977, and spent 19 years as team-mates, playing in an American League–record 1,918 games together. Over that span, the combo recorded more than 1,200 double plays.

"THE PLAYERS MAKE THE MANAGER, IT'S NEVER THE OTHER WAY."

—Sparky Anderson

# 85 Sparky Anderson

Anderson is the winningest manager in Tigers history and one of the best ever in the annals of major-league baseball. After leading the Cincinnati Reds to consecutive world championships in 1975 and 1976, Anderson was fired by the Reds following back-to-back second-place finishes in 1977 and 1978. The Tigers hired Anderson in June 1979, and his leadership paid immediate dividends as a lackluster team began to turn things around. By 1984, he had built a powerhouse team that went on to win the fourth World Series title in Tigers' history, making Anderson the first manager ever to win championships with teams from both leagues. Anderson's teams won 2,194 games, ranking fifth most of all-time among major-league managers, including 1,331 wins in his 17 years with the Tigers. Beloved by players and fans alike, Anderson temporarily left the Tigers in 1995 when he refused to manage a roster filled with replacement players during a players' strike, and he retired when the season ended. Anderson was inducted into the National Baseball Hall of Fame in 2000.

# 86 Bergman's At Bat

Dave Bergman was a journeyman first baseman who joined the Tigers on the eve of the 1984 season, picked up in a trade that also brought closer Willie Hernandez to the Tigers from Philadelphia. After the team's epic 35–5 start, the Tigers lost six of nine and their lead was reduced to 4 1/2 games. On June 4, the Tigers faced second-place Toronto in a showdown on *Monday Night Baseball*. With the score tied at 3 in the tenth, two outs, and two men on base, Bergman stepped to the plate to face reliever Roy Lee Jackson. After working the count full, Bergman fouled off seven straight pitches. Finally, he connected, launching a game-winning three-run homer. The Tigers never again felt threatened by anyone in their division. Sparky Anderson described Bergman's feat as the greatest at bat he'd ever seen.

Kirk Gibson celebrates his three-run homer in Game 5 of the 1984 World Series.

# 87 The Beast from the East

The 1984 Detroit Tigers began the season by winning 35 of their first 40 games—a major-league record. "The Beast from the East" led the AL East division wire to wire, winning a team-record 104 games and finishing 15 games ahead of second-place Toronto.

Lance Parrish smacked 33 homers. Kirk Gibson added 27, Alan Trammell hit .314, and Jack Morris won 19 games. As a team, Detroit led the league in home runs (187), runs scored (829), and team ERA (3.49). After sweeping the Kansas City Royals for the American League pennant, the Tigers returned to the World Series for the first time since 1968. Detroit edged the San Diego Padres in Game 1, 3–2, behind the pitching of Morris. San Diego evened the Series in Game 2, but the Tigers won Game 3, 5–2, behind Milt Wilcox, then rode Morris to a 4–2 win in Game 4. Remarkably, Detroit led the Series 3 games to 1 despite not having scored a single run after the fifth inning in any game. That all changed in Game 5. Leading 4–3 after six innings, the Tigers tacked on a run in the seventh to take a 5–3 lead. The Padres closed to 5–4 in the top of the eighth, but Gibson ended the drama with a towering three-run blast in the bottom of the frame, his second of the game, to clinch the Tigers' fourth World Series title and cement the 1984 Tigers' place in history.

# 88 The Big Wheel

Lance Parrish always pushed himself to get stronger and better. With an impressive physique chiseled from hours of strength training, Parrish applied that same approach to his baseball skills, and over time he became one of the best catchers ever to sport the Olde English D. Known as "the Big Wheel" for his ability to get things rolling, Parrish hit 22 or more home runs for five straight years, from 1982 to 1986. His 32 homers in 1982 broke Yogi Berra's AL record for catchers, which Parrish then topped in 1984 when he hit 33. In his 10 seasons with the Tigers, Parrish made the All-Star team six times and won three consecutive Gold Gloves from 1983 to 1985. Since retiring in 1995, Parrish has done two tours as a coach with the Tigers and also spent time in the broadcast booth.

# 89 Kirk Gibson

No one was more clutch than Kirk Gibson. He lived for the big moment, the pressure situations. His intensity and drive made everyone around him better. Gibson hit .282 with 27 home runs and 91 RBI in 1984, and he became the first Tiger to hit 20 homers and steal 20 bases in the same season, but he's probably best remembered for one of the most dramatic home runs in Tigers history. In Game 5, with two men on in the bottom of the eighth inning and the Tigers leading San Diego 5–4, Goose Gossage elected to pitch to Gibson instead of issuing him a free pass to an open first base. Gibson launched Gossage's offering into the upper deck of Tiger Stadium, sealing the Tigers' win and bringing another world championship to Detroit.

# 90 Jack Morris

Morris was ferociously competitive and often rubbed folks the wrong way, but that competitive fire drove him to be one of the best ever to pitch for Detroit. From the time he became a regular starter in 1979 through his final season with the club in 1990, Morris posted 15 or more wins 10 times. He won 20 games in 1983, then 19 more in 1984, including a no-hitter versus the White Sox on April 7, leading the Tigers to the AL pennant and a berth in the World Series. A classic big-game pitcher, Morris posted victories in Games 1 and 4, as the Tigers easily defeated the San Diego Padres 4 games to 1. He made 11 consecutive opening day starts for the Tigers, and his 198 wins with the Tigers rank fifth all-time. Morris also tallied 1,980 strikeouts while in Detroit, second best behind Mickey Lolich.

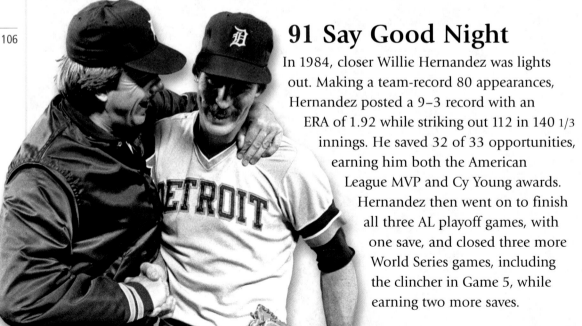

# 91 Say Good Night

In 1984, closer Willie Hernandez was lights out. Making a team-record 80 appearances, Hernandez posted a 9–3 record with an ERA of 1.92 while striking out 112 in 140 1/3 innings. He saved 32 of 33 opportunities, earning him both the American League MVP and Cy Young awards. Hernandez then went on to finish all three AL playoff games, with one save, and closed three more World Series games, including the clincher in Game 5, while earning two more saves.

Willie Hernandez and Lance Parrish celebrate winning the 1984 World Series. Opposite: Milt Wilcox and Jack Morris

## 92 Pizza Time

Longtime Tigers owner John Fetzer handpicked pizza giant Tom Monaghan, owner of Domino's Pizza, to replace him in 1983. The Tigers won a World Series for Monaghan in his first year of ownership, but financial woes forced him to sell the team in 1992. And who bought the ball club? Mike Ilitch, owner of the Little Caesar's chain of pizza restaurants.

## 93 Now or Later

Year after year, teams adopt a win-now philosophy, often sacrificing young, unproven talent for seasoned veterans. In 1987, with the Tigers unexpectedly in the race for the AL East title, they traded a minor-leaguer to Atlanta for soon-to-be 37-year-old veteran right-hander Doyle Alexander. The trade was successful for the Tigers. Alexander went 9–0 down the stretch, as the Tigers swept the final three games of the season from the Toronto Blue Jays to steal the AL East crown. Who'd they trade away for the title? John Smoltz, who through 2008 had won 210 games for the Braves.

## 94 Big Daddy

Cecil Fielder was a mountain of a man with a big teddy bear personality. Fielder swatted homers at a ridiculous rate during his seven-year stint in Detroit, including 51 in 1990 and 44 in 1991. He led the American League in RBI for three consecutive seasons, from 1990 to 1992, tying Babe Ruth's record. All told, the man affectionately known as "Big Daddy" smacked 245 home runs for the Tigers, ranking him fifth all-time, and drove in 758 runs. He's the only Tiger ever to hit 25 or more home runs in seven consecutive seasons and the first to hit one over the left-field roof in Tiger Stadium.

Cecil Fielder

# 95 Comerica Park

After more than 100 years at "The Corner" of Michigan and Trumbull, the Tigers moved into a new home in 2000. Comerica Park, in downtown Detroit, is built around family entertainment, not just the game itself. It seats nearly 42,000 fans and includes a carousel, Ferris wheel, and water feature in center field. A Walk of Fame presents a decade-by-decade history of baseball in Detroit along the main concourse, and statues of Tigers greats Ty Cobb, Charlie Gehringer, Hank Greenberg, Willie Horton, Al Kaline, and Hal Newhouser grace the concourse in left-center field. A giant scoreboard towers over the left-field bleachers, and there are no upper-level seats in center field, allowing patrons a view of downtown Detroit.

## 96 Home Run Derby

In a June 20, 2000, matchup with the Blue Jays in Toronto, the Tigers smacked a club-record eight home runs and crushed the Jays 18–6.

## 97 Halter Tops

On October 1, 2000, Shane Halter played all nine positions in one game—only the fourth player in major-league history to do that. He walked the only batter he faced while pitching in the eighth inning, got four hits, and scored the winning run in a 12–11 triumph over Minnesota.

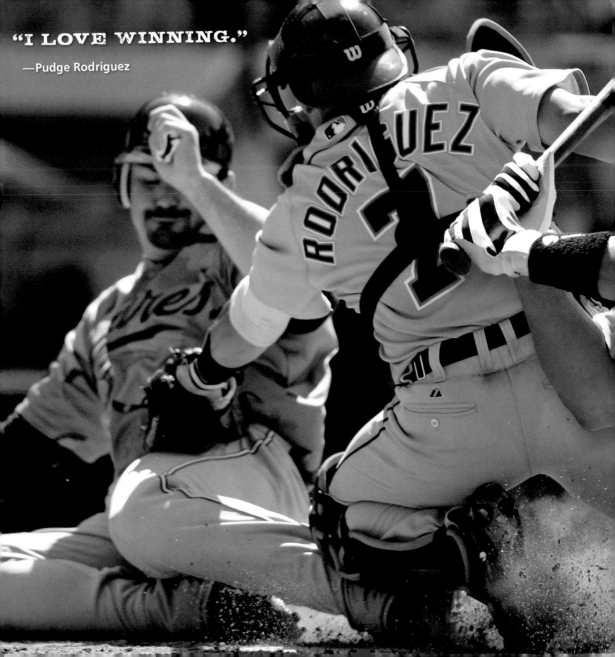

"I LOVE WINNING."

—Pudge Rodriguez

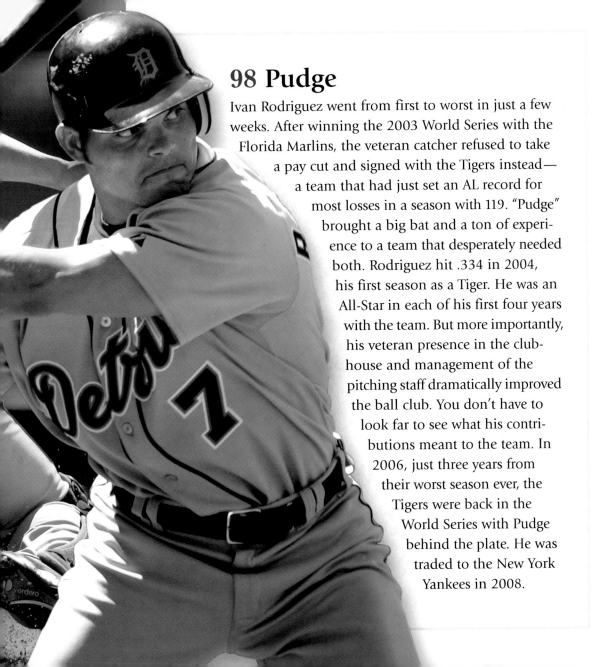

# 98 Pudge

Ivan Rodriguez went from first to worst in just a few weeks. After winning the 2003 World Series with the Florida Marlins, the veteran catcher refused to take a pay cut and signed with the Tigers instead— a team that had just set an AL record for most losses in a season with 119. "Pudge" brought a big bat and a ton of experience to a team that desperately needed both. Rodriguez hit .334 in 2004, his first season as a Tiger. He was an All-Star in each of his first four years with the team. But more importantly, his veteran presence in the clubhouse and management of the pitching staff dramatically improved the ball club. You don't have to look far to see what his contributions meant to the team. In 2006, just three years from their worst season ever, the Tigers were back in the World Series with Pudge behind the plate. He was traded to the New York Yankees in 2008.

"I KNEW IT WAS GONE AS SOON AS I HIT IT."

—Magglio Ordoñez

Magglio Ordoñez celebrating his game- and series-winning home run in the 2006 ALCS Opposite: Jim Leyland holding the American League championship trophy

# 99 A Return to Glory

The Tigers needed a fresh start. The storied franchise had been floundering for years. So fiery veteran manager Jim Leyland was brought in to turn things around in 2006. An early-season Leyland tirade lit a fire under the team, and they surged to the top of the AL Central, peaking at 40 games over .500 (76–36) in early August. Detroit stumbled badly down the stretch, handing the Central Division title to the Minnesota Twins, but the Tigers earned a spot in the playoffs as the wild card. Under Leyland's leadership, Detroit ripped off seven straight playoff wins to advance to the World Series, where they were defeated by the St. Louis Cardinals in five games. Leyland was named the AL Manager of the Year.

# 100 Magglio's Moment

The Tigers already had knocked the mighty New York Yankees out of the 2006 playoffs with a 3-games-to-1 triumph in the AL Division Series. And they had taken a surprising 3-games-to-none lead over the Oakland Athletics in the ALCS. With Game 4 knotted 3–3 in the bottom of the ninth, on the 22nd anniversary of the Tigers' last World Series triumph, Magglio Ordoñez stepped to the plate with a chance to send the Tigers back to the World Series. And with one mighty swing of the bat, Ordoñez launched a no-doubt three-runshot into the left-field seats that instantly washed away years of frustration and had Detroit celebrating once again.

Jim Northrup receives congratulations from teammates after his grand slam in Game 6 of the 1968 World Series.

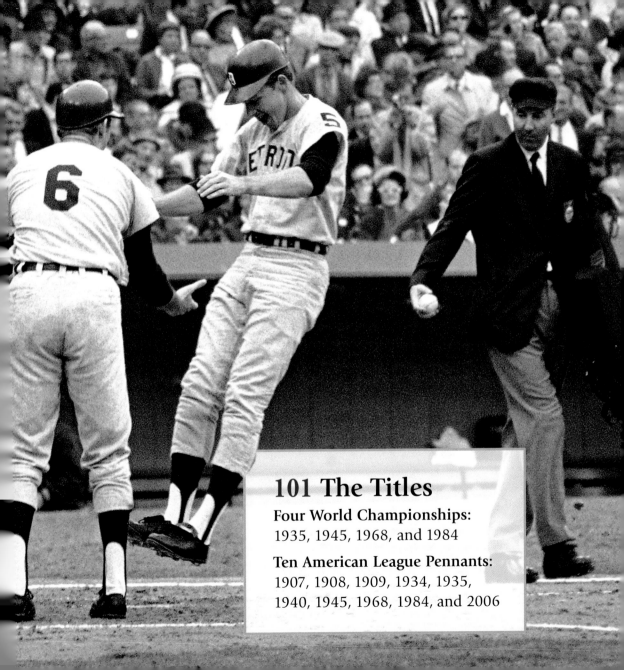

## 101 The Titles

**Four World Championships:**
1935, 1945, 1968, and 1984

**Ten American League Pennants:**
1907, 1908, 1909, 1934, 1935,
1940, 1945, 1968, 1984, and 2006

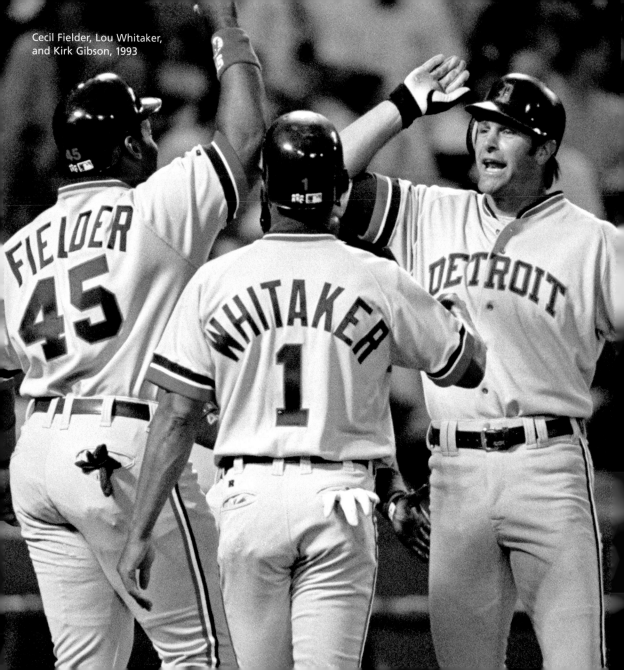

Cecil Fielder, Lou Whitaker,
and Kirk Gibson, 1993

# Acknowledgments

First and foremost, to the Detroit Tigers and all their fans, thanks for providing us with such a rich history to work with. And a huge thanks to Tigers fan Brice Anderson, who was an invaluable resource in putting this all together.

For providing me with this wonderful opportunity, a million thanks to my friend and mentor, Mary Tiegreen, and her husband, Hubert Pedroli, my golf buddy.

To my father, Ron Green Sr., and my brother, Ron Jr., thanks for the inspiration and guidance. You're the two best writers I know. Everyone should have the pleasure of reading your commentaries on sports and life on a daily basis. And to the rest of my family, thank you for your continuing love and support. You're the best.

To my home team, Mary, Savannah, Dakota, and Sam, I am blessed to have you in my life. Thanks for putting up with the curmudgeon who sometimes possesses me.

A special word of thanks goes out to the folks who provide the wonderful photographs you see in these books: Ted Ciuzio at AP Images, Pat Kelly at the National Baseball Hall of Fame Library, Jan Lovell of the *Detroit News* photography department, and Jake Novak. Your contributions are what make these books so special.

Lastly, to all the folks at Stewart, Tabori & Chang who had a hand in producing this book—specifically Ann Stratton and Jennifer Levesque —many, many thanks for all your effort and support. It is truly a pleasure working with you both. And to Richard Slovak, our copy editor extraordinaire, we couldn't do it without you.

119

**A Tiegreen Book**

Published in 2009 by Stewart, Tabori & Chang
An imprint of Harry N. Abrams, Inc.

Stewart, Tabori & Chang books are available at special discounts when purchased in quantity for premiums and promotions as well as fundraising or educational use. Special editions can also be created to specification. For details, contact specialmarkets@hnabooks.com.

Library of Congress Cataloging-in-Publication Data:

Green, David, 1959-
  101 reasons to love the Tigers /
  by David Green.
    p. cm.
    ISBN 978-1-58479-756-2

1. Detroit Tigers (Baseball team)—Miscellanea. I. Title.
  II. Title: One hundred one reasons to love the Tigers.
  III. Title: One hundred and one reasons to love the Tigers.

GV875.D6G694 2009
796.357'640977434—dc22
2008033593

Text copyright © 2009 David Green
Compilation copyright © 2009 Mary Tiegreen

Editor: Ann Stratton
Designer: David Green, Brightgreen Design
Production Manager: Tina Cameron

101 Reasons to Love the Tigers is a book in the 101 REASONS TO LOVE™ series.

101 REASONS TO LOVE™ is a trademark of Mary Tiegreen and Hubert Pedroli.

Printed and bound in China
10 9 8 7 6 5 4 3 2 1

**HNA** ▮▮▮▮▮
**harry n. abrams, inc.**
a subsidiary of La Martinière Groupe

115 West 18th Street
New York, NY 10011
www.hnabooks.com

**Photo Credits**

Pages 1, 10–11, 12–13, 22–23, 25, 30, 33 (portrait), 36–37, 37 (portrait), 39, 41, 42, 45, 46, 48, 52, 54, 57, 58, 59 (portrait), 60, 63, 64, 66–67, 69, 70 (portrait), 71, 72–73, 74 (inset), 74–75, 77, 78–79, 81, 82–83, 84, 86, 87 (portrait), 88–89, 90–91, 92, 95, 96 (portrait), 97, 99, 100, 102–103, 105, 106 (inset), 107, 109, 112, 113 (portrait), 114, 115 (inset), 116–117, and 118 courtesy of AP Images.

Pages 2–3 and 50–51 courtesy of the National Baseball Hall of Fame Library.

Pages 5, 6–7, 14, 16, 18 (cards), 20 (inset), 21, 26, 28 (card), and 32-33 courtesy of the Library of Congress Prints and Photographs department.

Pages 8-9 and 29 courtesy of the Detroit News.

Pages 34 (card), 35 (card), 56 (program), 62 (card), 65 (card), 80 (ball), 98 (card), and 120 (card) courtesy of David Green, Brightgreen Design.

Pages 110–111 courtesy of Jake Novak.

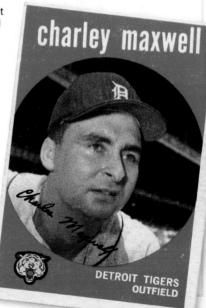